A Simple Way To Preach

Delmer Chilton and John Fairless

ISBN: 1491242248
ISBN-13: 978-1491242247

DEDICATION

Over fifteen years ago, we decided to get together on a regular basis to discuss the Lectionary texts. There is nothing unusual about that; there are "pericope study groups" all over the United States. What was different about this is that it was intentionally ecumenical by design.

Once a month we gathered in a classroom at Brook Hollow Baptist Church in the West Meade neighborhood of Nashville, TN: an Evangelical Lutheran, a couple of Cooperative Baptists, a United Methodist, a Disciple of Christ and a Presbyterian – perhaps an unlikely cohort, if not a motley crew.

We gathered with texts and resources and poured ourselves into being a community of truth as we pored over these words of truth together. Although most of us moved on to various places after a while, the community we created in that room proved to be "true church" for each of us in various times of trial, and the work we did together has led directly to the Lectionary Lab blog and the writing of this book.

The Bubbas therefore dedicate this volume to our colleagues and friends in the "Back Room Bible Club."

Contents

A Simple Way to Preach

ACKNOWLEDGMENTS

Our teachers have been many; some have been great, some have been good, and some probably wished they had been somewhere else besides the classroom. However, we are grateful for them all, for they have taught us to love words, to search for meaning, and never to rest until our work was done truly and well.

We are grateful for the use of the texts of scripture from the New Revised Standard Version. Copyright 1989, Division of Christian Education of the National Council of the Churches of Christ in the United States of America. Used by permission. All rights reserved.

Ideas and words from important authors are credited within the pages of the text. If we have missed anybody, we are truly sorry; please contact us and we will quickly repent of our foolish ways and seek to make amends as quickly as possible!

Support for this publication has been provided by the Billy Bob Bodine Junior High School for Biblical Studies and the Institute for the Consumption of Hickory Smoked Barbecue – both headquartered in Parts Unknown, Texas.

A Simple Way to Preach

Introduction

For those of you who know us, you already understand our **Two Bubbas and a Bible** approach to things. For those we haven't met (yet), a word may be in order.

Delmer Chilton (aka, Bubba #1) grew up in Appalachia on a farm that straddled the Virginia/North Carolina line— while John Fairless (Bubba #2) hails from the flatlands of West Tennessee. You probably don't need us to fill in any other details to figure out where "Bubba" comes in to our lived experience.

We met in Nashville, Tennessee several years ago when we were pastors (within our respective Lutheran and Baptist traditions) in the West Meade area of that city. Actually, we met as the dads of two seventh-grade boys on a field trip to the zoo...but, that's another story.

Friendship and partnership have ensued over the years, and in 2010, we began co-writing **The Lectionary Lab**, a weekly resource for lectionary preachers and other interested parties (we initially imagined our mothers would read us – and maybe a couple of other friends.)

It turned out that folks did read our stuff – and someone suggested we have a retreat for preachers to talk about the texts and the preaching task. So, we did…and we threw out a few suggestions that we had found helpful. Well, we've done that a few times now, and every time we hear things like, "Other preachers need to know what you're doing," and "You really ought to write this stuff up." So we did.

This book aims to be just exactly what the title says – *A Simple Way to Preach*.

(Our thanks and acknowledgement, by the way, go to Martin Luther for his brief work, *A Simple Way to Pray*.)

Since we are somewhat fond of stories, one of our favorites also says a lot about what we're trying to accomplish.

> *It seems that Delmer, while in seminary, was the preacher for a while at a fairly small, rural church in his beloved North Carolina. Most of you have been there – if not actually in North Carolina, then in your own state and your own setting – a small, "family" church – which of course means that there's somebody that pretty much runs things.*

> *In this case, there was a matriarch that needed pleasing, and Delmer certainly tried his best with his first sermon. After church, standing at the door to greet the parishioners, the head lady came on out and pronounced her sentence: "We're gonna' like you here. You're simple-minded, just like us!"*

There's nothing radically new here, as both of us have been influenced by some good teachers and preachers whose ideas (credited when we can remember where we heard them) appear as part of our work. We've also added our own insights from a combined 50+ years of "doing it" – preaching week in and week out. There's no task quite like that facing the working pastor. There are some folks that think that's an oxymoron, but we KNOW better!

Our aim is always to write things that will help our sisters and brothers who are on the field and in the pulpit each week. We know that you are busy and hard-pressed for time and inspiration. As we often say, "Sunday sure does roll around!" So, here are some thoughts on how you can go about the task of praying, planning, preparing, and preaching sermons. That's it.

We hope you find our little book "simple-minded," in its own way. It is, after all, just like us!

Chapter One: Working with Texts

In order to sustain a week-after-week rhythm of preaching to a congregation, a pastor must have time – and dedicate time – to study. The example from scripture is clear: "Study to show thyself approved unto God...," 1 Timothy 2:15 in the King James Version of our youth! And the practice of preachers over the course of a couple of thousand years is evidence that there is no easy path to preaching excellence.

Good sermons rarely – if ever – just happen!

So, how does one go about getting the most out of time in the study – especially when there are so many other things that the pastor may be called upon to tend to during a busy week?

Well, here's a **five-part process** that has worked well for us; the more you use it, the more the steps in the process go together and feed off of one another. But, in order to learn and practice – it helps to take it a step at a time.

Step 1: Start with the text

This may sound over-obvious, but there is sometimes a tendency to rush too quickly to see what your favorite preacher, commentator, or professor has to say **about** a text. The best place to start is **with** the actual text – the whole text and nothing but the text!

Whether you prefer to have your leather-bound Bible open in front of you, or to pull up the lessons for the day online, the point is to get the text in front of your face.

Once you have the text(s) before you, **pause to breathe and pray**; this opens your mind and body to the presence of the Spirit who guided the text into existence. We happen to think that it's always a good idea to hear a little something from the original Author, if you can.

Eli's advice to young Samuel in the temple could serve as a simple prayer: **"Speak, Lord, for your servant is listening."** (1 Samuel 3:10)

Words from a psalm such as **119:105** ("**Your word is a lamp unto my feet, and a light unto my path**....") could work, or even a text to a hymn or worship song. Basically, pray in any way that is good for you – but pray.

Read through the text once, just reading it – not stopping to notice any "points" or ideas for the sermon. Just begin getting the words into your mind, heart, and spirit. Then go back and read it again. Maybe even try it aloud.

After reading the text through at least twice, **then** begin paying attention to what the text says.

- What do you notice? Are there words, phrases, ideas that stand out to you?
- Are there things in this text that you don't quite understand? (This is a good time to mark those for further research in a later step.)
- Are there any places where this text upsets or bothers you? Are there ideas here that bring you comfort or some understanding?
- Is there anything odd or unusual or noteworthy in any other way?

Basically, you are just trying to let the text do its work in you — which may assume any number of forms. Again, don't worry too much about any kind of outline or plan for your sermon at this point — just pay attention to the shape and "texture" of the text. Jot a few notes to consider later.

Step 2: Think about God

No, this is not the time to plan the children's sermon questions, where every answer turns out to be "God" somehow. This is doing theology — speaking **words about God**. Since this is a Bible text, it most likely says something about God.

We're trying to ask a very important question: "Where is God in this text?"

- What do we learn from this text about God? God's character, nature, etc.?

- Does this fit with my previous ideas about God? Or, is there something different here?
- Are there any tension points with what we know from other texts, other ideas we have formed about God?
- How does this text impact our theological "world view" or fit our system? In fact, **does** it fit our system... or does it "upset the apple cart" or otherwise "blow our minds?"

We try not to move too far into planning and preparing a sermon **until we can answer this question** in some way. What does the text say to me – and, hence, what will I say to the congregation – about God?

Step 3: How is this text heard?

This is the **context** question.

How was this heard in the original community? You may need to dig a little in a commentary or other resource at this point. What was the perspective of the "readers" and "hearers" of these words? What was going on in the mind of the "preacher" or author of the text? What issues were they concerned with?

Next, you want to think about how this text will be heard in **your** context, **your** community. The same questions you asked about the original hearers are valid for your congregation members, too. What's going on in their lives that will situate this text in their minds? What are your concerns for them as you read and preach on this text?

You are moving now to the stage of **interpretation**. You are digging out of the text the important elements for your time and place. What the text says to one group of folks may not necessarily be exactly the same thing that will be meaningful for another group of folks at a different time and place.

This is also a great time to go back to the notes you jotted in **Step 1**; what questions did you have when you first read the text? Search for some answers to those. Are there particular words that intrigued or puzzled you?

Get some word study going on; see the **Appendix** for some recommendations and resources if it has been a while (or never) since you brushed up on your Hebrew and Greek!

Hermeneutics...now there's what we used to call a "highfalutin'" word!

But that's what you're thinking about here.

Hermeneutics is all about the way words are heard and function in a particular setting. The word *fight*, for example – may be a negative thing to be avoided, or a positive thing to encourage people to do (depending on the setting.)

> "Don't fight over the toys, children; there are enough for both of you."

"You've got to learn to stand up and fight for what is right."

What is the **listening situation** (hermeneutic) in your worship space on Sunday? In other words, how will the people to whom you preach hear this text and your words?

Step 4: Consider the "connection" to real life

This is the time to think of **illustration**.

The question is, "**Where does this connect to the *real world*?**" Are there situations that will help people understand or feel something in relation to this text? The situation and feelings could be positive or negative, humorous or serious – in some cases, they could even be tragic or graphic – though such illustrations must ALWAYS be used with great care!

Does the illustration you want to use contribute anything to the understanding of the text? Does it help to move the sermon forward? Or, is it just "a good story." Not every good story makes a good illustration, by the way. (More on this later, friends.)

Another important consideration here is, **"Where do good stories come from?"** We are in agreement with Dr. Frank Lewis, pastor of The First Baptist Church in Nashville, Tennessee, who says that, "The best stories come from life! Yours, mine, and ours...."

There are good stories going on all around you, every day. Learn to pay attention to what is happening in the world, and in your little town.

Parker Palmer (another of our favorite authors/thinkers/speakers) says that we must learn to "listen to our lives." Just paying attention will bring lots of ideas to your mind, once you begin to be aware. Some of the illustrations that open up the text will come from your own life – again, a technique to use with care (and one that is also covered in the next chapter.)

When you think about it, this is what Jesus did so often in his sermons and parables. He took very common, everyday objects and situations and used them for teaching spiritual ideas.

With just a little practice, you will be amazed at the connections you can form from your own experience and that of the community you serve. We're going to work through each of these steps in an exercise at the end of the chapter, and we'll show you what we mean by learning to listen to your life.

This step is all about **situating the text** in our experience; life gives the text a frame of reference. Of course, a case can be made that it is **the text that situates our experience** and gives the frame of reference for life. We like it either way!

Step 5: Start putting it all together

Now we are ready to build a sermon! (Sort of...)

As you begin to construct the sermon, the best advice we can give is ... **don't rush it!** This is the time to let the ideas and discoveries – even the questions you may still have – come together into a form.

What has begun to take shape in your mind? Are there key points or ideas that you believe the text is emphasizing? Are there elements here that will speak particularly to the people in your pews? Have you decided on a key illustration (or possibly two – but probably not more?)

This is where you take three very important actions:

- *Visual*-**ize**... see what it is you want to say, as well as what you want to occur before, during, and after your sermon. This may not be a distinct vision, or even words; it is more of an idea. You can begin to sense the direction you want to take.

- *Form*-**alize**... see the flow and order of your thoughts and ideas. Put them into a grid, an outline, a chart, a paragraph – whatever works for you. One great suggestion we have used at this point is to begin with a clear statement – **in just one sentence** – of the sermon's main idea. What do I want people to have experienced when the sermon is over? Think about this until you know it for yourself.

- ***Aural*-ize** – begin to actually speak the words and phrases you will use. Read your notes or your manuscript aloud, so that it falls on your own ears before you ever try to present it to others. Sometimes, your ears will hear things that your eyes didn't catch – both good and bad!

Now, start putting it down. Both of us Bubbas believe in the power of **writing out a word-for-word manuscript** in order to get your thoughts into their clearest possible expression. You may or may not actually use the manuscript when you preach, but it remains the best tool you have for getting focused in what you want to say.

Stick with the discipline of writing – and writing well!

Write, re-write, practice, prepare, pray (again) ...let the rhythm of your week flow as you work each day on the sermon. (Yes, it is a good idea to start early in the week and do a little something every day. "Saturday night specials" are a part of every pastor's experience – especially if you've had a couple of funerals and lots of hospital visitation in a particular week. But don't make them a regular occurrence – please.)

Find and follow the rhythm that works for you. It is **your** voice that God intends to use to speak the word of the Lord on Sunday.

You can't preach like somebody else; you can only preach like you. But that will be perfectly fine and acceptable. God has called **you** to these people and this pulpit.

Isn't it amazing, that after all these years, God still chooses **"by the foolishness of preaching to save those who believe?"** (1 Corinthians 1:21)

In the next chapter, we'll take a look at what putting these steps into practice might look like.

Chapter Two: Using the Five-Part Process

Let's see how the process we outlined in the previous chapter works with an actual text from scripture.

We're going to use as an example Mark 2:13-22, the gospel reading for the **8ᵗʰ Sunday after the Epiphany** (one of the Sundays preceding Lent**)** or **Proper 3** (one of the Sundays after Pentecost) **in Year B**; this text will actually not be read again until at least 2018, but it will give us an idea of what it's like to work with a "real" lectionary text.

Step 1 involves reading the text – at least two times – without any other aids or study materials in front of us. So, let's start with that. (We like to read it silently one time, then go back and read it aloud.)

Mark 2:13-22 (NRSV)
2:13 Jesus went out again beside the sea; the whole crowd gathered around him, and he taught them.

2:14 As he was walking along, he saw Levi son of Alphaeus sitting at the tax booth, and he said to him, "Follow me." And he got up and followed him.

A Simple Way to Preach

2:15 And as he sat at dinner in Levi's house, many tax collectors and sinners were also sitting with Jesus and his disciples--for there were many who followed him.

2:16 When the scribes of the Pharisees saw that he was eating with sinners and tax collectors, they said to his disciples, "Why does he eat with tax collectors and sinners?"

2:17 When Jesus heard this, he said to them, "Those who are well have no need of a physician, but those who are sick; I have come to call not the righteous but sinners."

2:18 Now John's disciples and the Pharisees were fasting; and people came and said to him, "Why do John's disciples and the disciples of the Pharisees fast, but your disciples do not fast?"

2:19 Jesus said to them, "The wedding guests cannot fast while the bridegroom is with them, can they? As long as they have the bridegroom with them, they cannot fast.

2:20 The days will come when the bridegroom is taken away from them, and then they will fast on that day.

2:21 "No one sews a piece of unshrunk cloth on an old cloak; otherwise, the patch pulls away from it, the new from the old, and a worse tear is made.

2:22 And no one puts new wine into old wineskins; otherwise, the wine will burst the skins, and the wine is lost, and so are the skins; but one puts new wine into fresh wineskins."

Did you actually take the time to read – **twice?**

If you didn't, we're going to say this only one time: **do not rush this part of the process**, no matter how many times you have read the text before, or how well you think you know it. We promise you, there is always more lurking there than you have imagined – and you just never know when a fresh idea is waiting for you to see it.

Okay, here ends the lesson!

Now, we want to begin looking back through the text, noting things that stand out to us. They can be words, phrases, ideas, questions, things we need to mark for further study, things that confuse us or inspire us or just plain seem a little odd to us.

(We actually like to print the passage out on its own page, with space in between the verses, so that we can circle and underline and make notes as they come to us.

Accessing the Revised Common Lectionary website at http://lectionary.library.vanderbilt.edu makes this process a snap!)

What we immediately notice is that there is a whole crowd following Jesus, listening to his teaching. This is not the first time he has addressed a crowd, evidently, since v. 1 says he went out "again." What does the "again" refer to? (You'll want to check that later...)

Almost incidentally to his teaching, he "sees" Levi sitting by the way, collecting taxes. Jesus decides to call this Levi fellow to follow him. Why? We're not sure (yet), but Levi's response is immediate. He not only gets up to follow Jesus, he invites him home for dinner.

There's a big crowd of Levi's acquaintances that come along and join the party; these are apparently some "unsavory" types, according to the good religious folks of the day – noted here as "the scribes of the Pharisees." (This is another term we may want to check on later.)

Jesus next pops out with some proverbial wisdom about well folks not needing a doctor; this obviously has something to do with the situation, and identifies something of his purpose and ministry. He is looking for "sinners" to help out; righteous people need not apply (reminds us of the 70's song, "Signs," by the *Five Man Electrical Band* – which we may also check out later.)

We finish up with another little religious ditty about fasting – other gangs of disciples are fulfilling their religious duty to abstain from food and wine, but Jesus' crew shows no such propensity. Why?

Again, Jesus has an answer – this time set in the context of a wedding party rejoicing with the bridegroom, who will not be around for long. After the reason for the party has gone, Jesus says, there will be plenty of time for glum faces.

The oddest part of the passage is the conclusion; we've got to do some thinking about this "new wine, old wineskins" stuff. So, we'll write that up as a question to be considered later.

Well, that's it for this stage; again, your point is not so much to think these ideas through to their conclusion just yet. You are simply trying to notice what's going on. You'll take time to figure it out later.

If you try to go too deep at this point, you are likely to miss some detail that may bear fruit for you later. So, **put aside the urge to figure it all out** at this stage, and just keep reading and paying attention.

When you've noticed everything that you feel you can, move on to **Step 2.**

Put aside the urge to figure it all out at this stage, and just keep reading and paying attention.

Step 2 is thinking theologically – what does this text say about God? What do I learn about God – if anything – from this passage?

To be real honest, this is not one of the more overtly theological passages that we have to deal with. We mostly notice the connection here to *sin*, which is certainly a good theological word. The Bible uses it quite regularly to talk about the way we have become separated, or alienated, from God and from the purposes of God.

We probably would like to check the language used here for *sin* and *sinner;* why are the Pharisees so concerned about the sinners, and why does Jesus say he has come to call for sinners?

For that matter, why **IS** he hanging out with this particular crowd on this day? What does Jesus' presence with "sinners" have to say about God and God's purpose for Jesus' life?

Now, we move on in to **Step 3** – starting to think about the context of this story.

We first notice that this is fairly early in the gospel of Mark; we are only in Chapter 2. Yet, since Mark's gospel moves so quickly and covers so much ground, we have seen quite a bit of Jesus' ministry already.

The passage for today comes just after a famous "controversy story" – in which Jesus forgives the sins of a crippled man and has him get up off his mat and walk away. (vv. 1-12)

That scene comes after the action-packed Chapter 1, in which Jesus is:

- baptized by John
- travels to the wilderness to be tempted by the devil
- reappears and picks up his preaching ministry where John (who is now in prison) left off
- walks the shore by the Sea of Galilee and begins to pick disciples
- moves his base of operation to Capernaum and preaches in the synagogue there
- casts an unclean spirit out of a man at the synagogue (we will resist any comments here about similarities to some of the church members we have known!)
- heals Simon's mother-in-law
- gets pressed by crowds who need similar healing
- has a very early-morning prayer session, then
- packs up his burgeoning band of followers and heads through the countryside for more preaching, teaching, and healing.

Whew! Jesus sure was busy!

Now all of that is the backstory for the scene we have today, as Jesus is apparently doing what he did every day – walking by the sea, talking to folks, and happening upon men that he thinks need to come and follow him – in this case, Levi.

That Levi is an unlikely candidate – from our external perspective – is signaled by the fact that he is a "tax collector." A little searching in commentaries (whether print or online) lets us know that this was a public office, connected with the Roman system of taxation to support the empire, and that pretty much all tax collectors were in the business of keeping a little extra for themselves – some, but not all, in order to maintain extravagant lifestyles. Reminds us of the story of Zacchaeus in Luke 19 – might want to reference that account.

An example of an online link you could use for this type of background can be found here: http://www.bible-history.com/taxcollectors/TAXCOLLECTORSHistory.htm

So, there's a bit of a scandal raised by Jesus in the simple act of his calling a tax collector to come and join him; the scandal is blown beyond all proportion when he attends a supper filled with tax collectors and other **sinners**.

It is too much for "the scribes of (sometimes - *and*) the Pharisees," a group which consistently represents the perspective of the good church folk of the day – the religious leadership who claimed to live their lives by the mandates of Scripture. They continue their questioning of Jesus' methods and motives – which had begun in the earlier part of the passage (see Mark 2:6.)

Three perspectives suggest themselves at this point:

- Jesus is obviously hoping to make some sort of point with his actions

- The scribes and Pharisees are trying to make sense/understand/seek to discredit what they see happening
- The people in the crowds are most likely aware of the underlying tension between Jesus and the religious leadership – and are wondering which way the tension will be resolved

It could be fruitful to consider to what extent – or, in what way, if any – these same tensions or perspectives might be present in our own setting.

Do we ever have any tensions in our congregations over religious practices – the ways they are implemented (or not)? Do we ever have discussions and/or disagreements over who is allowed to come in and to participate "fully" in the life of the church?

One cannot help but wonder if Jesus ever allows anything to happen in our midst today just to shake us up a little bit? Do we ever raise our eyebrows or our questions about the way we live life together in the church?

As far as the fasting and the wineskins piece – Jewish wedding customs formed the backdrop for several events in Jesus' life. John's gospel has the famous "wedding at Cana" water-into-wine story as Jesus' first miracle. There are some symbols here that might be worth paying attention to.

- Rejoicing is a central part of the life together that God calls us to

- When in the presence of God's mercy and grace (symbolized in forgiveness of sins/healing of a cripple, calling to service of a sinful tax collector) other distinctions (lines that we tend to draw?) begin to fade away

- "All" are welcome at the banquet, as far as Jesus is concerned

- New wine – new ways of seeing (as Levi is "seen" by Jesus) – will tend to stretch out old containers (the ferment causes the volume of gas to grow, technically speaking, and the old containers have already been stretched to their limits)

- In order to "see" God's new work in our midst, perhaps some new understandings and new practices will have to be considered – even if we like our perfectly acceptable and comfortable old wineskins

Finally, a key word we identified earlier was "**sinners**;" these people are the object of Jesus' mission. What is a sinner? And who are the sinners? They seem to be the people Jesus is most concerned about.

A little work on the Greek word used here – *hamartolos*, or *hamartolon* – allows us to see that this is a description of folks who have "missed the mark" or "strayed from the path." They are not going to get where they want to go – and, implied perhaps, where

God wants them to go – if they continue the way they are headed.

(Again, check the **Appendix** for some help with understanding biblical Greek and/or Hebrew.)

So, Jesus compares these sinners to people who are sick and need to see a doctor; they need guidance, care, help, or some medicine. Whatever else it is that they need, Jesus is certainly concerned that they change the course of the way that they are living.

From our study of the context (see above), we know that in Chapter 1, Jesus' message was the same as that of John the Baptist: "…repent, and believe the good news."

Repentance is all about change; literally, it's a word that means "stop going in one direction, and start going in another" (among other shadings, of course!)

Apparently, Jesus has come to tell and show people that there's a better way to live – and that it has something to do with forgiving sins, following Jesus, and being made whole.

Now, again we ask: just who are these sinners that Jesus has come to call? Oh, my goodness – **they might be us!**

Having followed up on most of the trails that

we set for ourselves in this process, it's time to move on to **Step 4.**

Step 4 involves finding the "connection" to real life for ourselves and our listeners. As a preacher, we must answer the question, "What is going to help me illustrate this text and help my people feel that it really is a story for them, too?"

A very simple illustration comes immediately to mind: we could ask, at or near the opening of our sermon, "How many people here have ever had a time where you knew you were about to do something that you shouldn't – maybe say something you knew you would later regret – and you went right ahead and did it anyway?"

(You will most likely get a number of heads nodded or even hands raised.)

We're getting a little simple buy-in to the fact that "missing the mark" or "straying from the path" is awfully easy to do.

Another way in to understanding some of the dynamics of this text is to play off of the poor tax collectors. Fair or not, most people in our time have a "low opinion" of the IRS (or other taxing agency in your location) and the role they play in placing their hands in our wallets. Of course, some of us have IRS employees in our congregations, so we need to be careful here!

Again, the point is to help people get a feel for the fact that Levi and his friends might not have won any popularity contests with most of the people of Jesus' day.

We might well play on what our listeners know (or think they know) about the Pharisees in the story. Lots of folks have heard enough Bible stories to know that **the Pharisees are often portrayed as the "bad guys"** – something of a foil for Jesus as he makes his point. No good, dramatic story ever succeeds without a villain to conquer or a problem to be solved. We'll talk a bit about that later.

These are the kinds of things we mean when we talk about "listening to life." There are almost always common experiences that can be called up within the sermon that have a bearing on a situation from the scriptural text.

What about "published stories" that can be found in books, on the internet, or in other sources? We have certainly used those – and still do, from time to time – again, the main qualification for any "illustration" is: does it move the purpose of the sermon forward? Does it make a contribution?

If it does, then by all means use it. If it's just a cute, funny, or moving story that doesn't really have anything to add to what you want people to know – probably best to save it for another time.

The main qualification for any "illustration" is: does it move the purpose of the sermon forward? Does it make a contribution?

Okay, then we're ready for **Step 5** – time to put some of these ramblings and musings together in a form.

As you can see, using the process can actually generate quite a bit of information. We now have several possible ideas for a sermon, and more "facts" than we can reasonably fit into our 10- or 20-minute format (or whatever your allotted time is.) So, we need to make some decisions.

As we back up a bit and begin to **visualize** what we want to see in this sermon, the images of joy and acceptance might begin to come through.

There was certainly a fair amount of rejoicing over the healing of the lame man that immediately preceded this story; there is evident rejoicing when Jesus joins Levi and his friends at home for supper; there is even the allusion to joy over the wedding feast with the bridegroom, as well as the implied joy of those who are sick and sinful being made whole, and being forgiven of sin and set back on the path to life.

If that is the image we choose to work with, then we look through our accumulated notes to see what "fits" in that vein. We begin to **formalize** the bits into an organized presentation.

Jesus is interested in bringing joy to the lives of those around him – though there are some in the stories who are being prevented from experiencing joy. There are a variety of things that hinder joy – things like illness, unclean spirits, the absence of loved ones (the bridegroom), and even questions/concerns/things that people are bothered about.

Jesus is in the business of removing those impediments – he is a healer, a cleanser and forgiver of sins, a person who values relationship, and a person who sees more value in people than in rules.

At the end of the story, we might well consider **who received joy from Jesus – and who did not**. Those willing to understand their need for healing and forgiveness received it; those who held on to their questions, their objections, their concerns and opinions about Jesus... did not.

Finally, we might bring this story "home" to our time – **does Jesus desire the same joy and acceptance for us?** Are there hindrances we face to receiving that joy and acceptance? If we do not receive the joy of Jesus – and share it with others – could that be because we are holding on to some things that we ought to consider letting go?

Now, this may be a bit oversimplified at this point, but we want to get the main image down to something very presentable and understandable. So, even if it's not in final form yet, this is the part of the process where we have to leave a good deal "on the cutting room floor," to borrow a phrase from the world of film editing.

Now we are ready to **auralize** this sermon – actually hear, either in our mind or aloud – how it is going to sound.

We see that we have developed four distinct movements, or **pivot points**, for the story we want to tell on this particular Sunday. We can begin to try those on for size – we can imagine the people that will sit in our pews this Sunday listening to these ideas. If they sound pretty good, and if they seem to fit the situation for our folks, good; we're ready to start writing in earnest.

If they need a little adjustment or reworking, good; now's the perfect time to make changes. Let your prayerful contemplation at this point open your heart and mind to the Spirit who has been guiding this process the entire way.

What we've just done is to take a text from the beginning point – starting with the text, and the text alone – and we've worked it through a process for thorough exploration and thought. While it may seem a bit daunting at first, we believe that once you've tried it a time or two, you will discover that the steps begin to fit together like a well-oiled machine.

What you will discover – we sincerely hope – is **a way to prepare for any sermon with any text on any occasion.** This is not hard, but it does take work. God bless you as you take it on!

In the next chapter, we'll consider some ways to actually fill these ideas out into a full-fledged sermon.

Chapter Three: How Sermons Work

It's All Narrative

One of the more important things we have learned over the years about preaching is that there is a basic pattern to the way sermons work. Some of them work well, others barely function, but all sermons work in the same basic way. **Creating better sermons is mostly a matter of working with the basic pattern instead of working against it.**

That basic pattern is narrative. This does not mean that sermons need to be written in the form of a story or that they should contain any other story than the biblical story.

It does mean that sermons are an art form that has more in common with storytelling than it does with essay-writing or philosophical argumentation.

Unfortunately, many preachers know more about the writing of essays or the making of arguments than they do about the telling of stories.

Again, it is important not to confuse narrative form with the telling of stories. They are not the same thing. We want to learn why people listen to well told stories and then craft our sermons in such a way that people will listen to them and experience them in much the same way they listen to and experience a story.

This is vital because when we get up to talk, people listen to us like we are storytellers and they seek to find out from us what they find out from storytellers. And we will tell them the things storytellers tell people. But, if we do not pay attention to structure, it will be more difficult for us to tell and for them to hear.

There is a basic formula for this sort of thing and it is used quite ably by people whose writing lives most resemble the work of a parish pastor: the TV script writer.

Week after week they use the same characters and basic themes to craft a new story that is calculated to hold people's attention. If they do their work well, you will not notice the formula; sometimes they do their work so exceptionally well that even if you notice the formula you don't care – it is done so compellingly.

That basic formula has **four steps**.

- Things go wrong.

- Things get worse while main character (or characters) tries to figure things out.

- The answer is arrived at.

- The results of the answer in the lives of the characters are explored.

Think about your basic episode from the popular show, "Law and Order."

Things go wrong. The opening scene is almost always a couple of innocent bystanders finding a body in gruesome circumstances.

Things get worse. The lead detectives chase down several dead-end leads, or they find that the story is more complicated than they thought.

The answer. By good police work, or luck, or some combination of the two, the detectives figure it out and arrest someone and hand the case over to the lawyers.

The results of the answer are explored. During the trial phase we see behind the scenes into the whys and wherefores of the crime and the way that crime and its resolution have changed everyone's life.

Now, let's transfer this idea to a sermon.

Before crafting a sermon, one has accumulated a mass of exegetical and hermeneutical data. Most of the time an idea has begun to germinate: a message, a point, a thing you want people to hear. The basic question is how do you get

The basic question is how do you get from that mass of data to that idea and its implications for people's lives?

from that mass of data to that idea and its implications for people's lives?

Sometimes we tell them the answer upfront, in the introduction, and then work our way logically through our biblical and theological material to show them why we need that answer, how it is to be arrived at, and how this answer changes our lives.

Sometimes we follow an exegetical outline, exploring and explaining the text, pointing out the problem and its solution along the way and then, in the "application" exploring the way this solution changes our lives.

These are not bad ways to preach, but they can be inefficient. They bring the techniques of academia, the essay and the lecture, into the pulpit -- where they are generally ill-suited to the task.

People are wired to listen for the basics of a "narrative" and they are usually there; they are just sometimes hard to find and follow. People carefully listen to find out three things:

1) What's the problem?

2) What's the answer?

3) What difference does it make?

Dealing directly with those questions in that basic order makes for easier listening and better preaching. We call this the **Listener's Three Questions**.

Eugene Lowry, in his 1970s book *The Homiletical Plot* was one of the first to set this out in a systematic way. He posited five basic movements:

- upsetting the equilibrium,

- analyzing the discrepancy,

- disclosing the clue to resolution,

- experiencing the gospel, and

- anticipating the consequences.

Our **Listener's Three Questions** formula covers the same ground in a simpler way. Listeners to a well-told story do not stand one step back from the problem and its growing complexity followed by its resolution.

When a story is properly told, **the problem has become personal and so the clue to resolution is personal as well**, and is experienced as a gospel moment of grace and release and freedom.

How Does It Work?

In the previous section we examined **Mark 2:13-22** using our five-step system for working with the text.

Take a few minutes to go back and review those pages along with your own insights. Looking over that data, ask yourself, "What's the problem?" "What is out of kilter?" "What arouses the curiosity, whether of people in the text or of people reading the text?"

There is an overall problem/question of "Who is this Jesus?" "What sort of Rabbi, teacher, Messiah is he?"

Answers to that question are complicated by his association with tax collectors and other sinners (vs. 13-17) and his community's failure to be ascetic like the followers of John the Baptizer and the Pharisees (vs. 18-20).

A basic presenting problem of the text is that Mark has positioned Jesus as the Messiah but Jesus has been acting in a very un-Messiah-like manner.

The answer/clue provided in the text is that God-in-Christ is doing a new thing and you cannot expect a new thing to fit an old model. Jesus illustrates this with his references to unshrunk cloth and new wine. (vs. 21-22)

One narrative possibility, based on our previous research, might go like this:

What's the problem?

"Why do the Pharisees think Jesus isn't very holy?" We go deeper into this question as Tax collectors, sinners, Pharisees, and disciples are briefly discussed and the story explained

What's the answer?

God, in Christ, is doing a new thing: physician for the sick, calling the sinner, unshrunk cloth and new wine

What difference does it make?

- We are all more like sick sinners than we are like righteous Pharisees

- The church, the body of Christ, is called to serve the sick, the outcast, the sinners

- God is always making old things new, and we must adjust our old cloth, our old wineskins, to receive new cloth and new wine.

Now you can begin developing the sections of the outline.

The most important and often the most difficult section to develop is the first half of "**What's the problem**?"

This is because these first 300 or 400 words not only set the problem to be resolved, they must also be calculated to **grab the listeners' attention** in such a way that their mind will not wander until the sermon is over.

This is where it is vital to relate the biblical world to our current context; vividly and from the very beginning. There is a two-pronged need here: to identify the question in the text; and to show that it matters to us, here, today in this place.

This first section is the place to be personal and somewhat conversational, inviting the congregation to look with you at the world around us.

Remember, this is the introduction to a narrative event and has more in common with the observational humor style of Jerry Seinfeld than it does with the telling of hilarious stories like Bill Cosby.

And it doesn't necessarily have to be funny. The key is to be both interesting and authentic while at the same time drawing people into the intersection of a question or problem in the biblical

It is vital to relate the biblical world to our current context

world and a similar question or problem in our own. For example, this could be an opening section for a sermon on this text:

I wouldn't be a teen-ager again for love nor money. I was talking with a friend who has children who are in high school. He recently moved across the country and his 10th grade son has been having difficulty fitting in, finding a place in the teen-age pecking order.

Listening to his story brought back my own memories of being on the outside looking in, of not being one of the popular kids, of being considered a little weird and strange; because I read books that I didn't have to read for one thing and I had no eye for fashion for another. I dressed not so much badly as oddly: scarves and blue blazers with painter's pants and orange Converse tennis shoes.

Most of us have found ourselves on the outside looking in at one time or another in our lives. And the person who matters most to us in those situations is the one who breaks down the unofficial barriers and invites us into the inner circle, the one who risks the scorn and rejection of those who matter in order to reach out to those who don't.

In our Gospel lesson for today, those standing on the outside looking in, those who were considered a little strange and unacceptable to those who mattered, were the "tax collectors and sinners," those who knew who was in and who was out were the Pharisees, and the one who was in but broke the circle and reached out to bring others in, was Jesus.

That last little paragraph beginning, "In our Gospel lesson . . ." provides **the bridge to begin exploring the question more deeply, looking about for an answer**.

This is a matter of exploring the difference between who the good people thought Jesus ought to be and who he really was. It is also a place to talk about the why the people Jesus chose to spend time with upset them so much. This is where a lot of the accumulated exegetical and hermeneutical data from our earlier process can be used.

One can quickly explore who the Pharisees were and what their expectations of others were and how they defined a **sinner**, and why **tax collectors** were lumped into that sinner pile.

This should be done with brief clarity, not diverting from the main plot of your sermon by wandering down rabbit-holes full of somewhat arcane details. Those belong in the classroom, not the sermon.

An important brief picture to draw is the contrast between the Messiah they expected and the one they received, and how difficult it was for them adjust their thinking. A brief version this portion might look a little like this:

> *Pharisees weren't actually the ogres we've managed to turn them into. They were a lot more like us modern church folk than most of the other people we read about in the Bible. A pretty good case could be made that Jesus himself was a Pharisee, in sympathy if not in fact. Pharisees were people who took God's word and holy living seriously.*

> *They were people who made an attempt to live each day as if they really meant the things they said in synagogue on the Sabbath. They looked around and saw many people whom they did not think took the faith as seriously as they ought. Some were indeed blatant, hard-hearted, evil sinners, most were simply ordinary folk who found it difficult to be as pure and holy and as observant as the Pharisees while at the same time trying to earn a living in an impure and often unholy world.*

And the tax collectors were a special case. The Romans ruled the known world, in most places directly, in others, like Israel, through puppet kings whom they propped up with Roman military power. The "tax collectors" were seen by the Pharisees as "collaborators with the enemy," and as corrupt besides, because the tax system was built on bribery and coercion and was anything but fair.

In the midst of this situation, the Pharisees had placed their hopes on their purity and obedience pleasing God is such a way that God would send the Messiah to remove the Roman boot from their necks and reestablish Israel as a holy nation. The fact that many thought Jesus might be that Messiah distressed them because his behavior in hanging out with the less than pure and the tools of the enemy was the exact opposite of what they thought the Messiah should be doing.

In our **Listener's Three Questions** outline, we have answered the first part: **What's the Question?**

The sermon is at the halfway point and it is time to turn the corner and go in a new direction. The listeners are ready to get some answers and if none are forthcoming, they will stop listening.

It is time to move to listener's question two – **"What's the answer?"**

It is essential that this move be clear and unambiguous. The connection between the question and its answer has to make theological and Biblical sense and must be stated with such clarity and simplicity that there can be no mistaking the meaning.

In creating this section, **careful adherence to what the text actually reveals about the answer is the key**. In this case, Jesus provides the answer in conversation with the Pharisees.

While there are essentially three answers given in the text, they all fall within the general answer that "God-in-Christ is doing a new thing which doesn't neatly fit within old categories."

> Careful adherence to what the text **actually** reveals about the answer is the key.

The way Mark has structured the text, there are two questions which receive somewhat direct answers; then Jesus makes a generalized statement about newness using two analogies – cloth and wine.

To fully explore the implications of all the answers and their images of doctors and patients and bridegrooms and weddings and unshrunk cloth and new wineskins would take too long and would confuse the listener.

This is the place for simplicity – those are questions to be explored more extensively in a teaching setting.

What we must do is hone in on the "God-in-Christ is doing a new thing" answer and lightly touch on the other answers as images, using them to make our point more clear, not less. This third section might look something like this:

It did not take Jesus long to find out that the people with whom he had the most in common were not happy with him.

Say what you will about the Pharisees, you did not have to wonder what was on their minds. If they had a problem with you, you knew about it, and you knew exactly what it was because they told you.

"Why do you eat with sinners?"

"Because it's the sick people who need a doctor."

"Why do your disciples not pray and fast like good holy people?"

"Because I'm with them now, when I'm dead and gone, then they'll fast and pray."

Seeing that his answers were not satisfying them, Jesus explains further. Jesus knows that he is not the type of Messiah they were looking for, he knows that his actions don't fit within their understanding of who he's supposed to be and how he's supposed to act. So he tries again. Using familiar and homespun images from around a normal house, mending clothes and storing wine, he pushes them to see that it is only normal that when God does a new thing that it will not fit easily and comfortably into an old pattern. The new cloth will tear the old coat, the new wine will expand and explode outside the old containers.

The simple truth of the Gospel is that when God does something new, everything changes and God's people must be ready to change with it. In Christ, God began to welcome into the community people who had previously been excluded.

In Christ, God invited the community to celebrate God's presence more and lament God's absence less. In Christ, God declared that new things were happening and that everything was changing.

The corner having been turned, the answer revealed, it is now time to pick up speed as we move into listener's question three – **"What difference does it make?"**

In this section it is important to return to our current context and, with simple clarity and something of a sense of urgency, spell out what this answer/clue means for us as individuals and as congregations and communities of faith. Here is one take at how this last section could look.

One of the most important things we can ask ourselves in reading a Biblical text is this, "Who in this story do I identify with?" Put a different way, "Who in this story feels the most like me?" While most of us wish we could say "Jesus," most of us know that's not likely to be true – well, not for most of us. We are much more likely to feel like one of the Pharisees, standing back and wondering why other people behave the way they do. Or,

It's even more likely that we feel like the "tax collectors and sinners," excluded and looked down upon by some group or the other. But how many of us identified ourselves as sick of spirit and in need of a physician of the soul? That's is who I have come to know myself as, and it is who I think most of us are; sinners in need of salvation, weak ones in need of being lifted up, hurting and wounded people in search of healing and relief.

And the good news is that Jesus the Messiah has come to bring all those things to us, and to everyone. Just as Jesus partied with the "tax collectors and sinners," and the Pharisees when they were willing, Jesus has come to party with us, to wine and dine, and hug and heal, and to make all things new, in us and through us.

For we have been invited to become a part of Jesus' not-so-exclusive supper club. All are invited, anyone can come and as we leave the table and the party we discover ourselves transformed from guests into hosts, from those who are hurting into those who are healing others, from those excluded into those who bring others in. It is our calling today to open ourselves up to the new wine of God's love in Christ, and to be prepared for things to change as we move into God's future together.

This sermon moves through a narrative arc without either telling a story external to the text or re-telling the Biblical story in the Biblical order with commentary.

Instead, it follows the order of our **Listener's Three Questions** to achieve a sermonic flow that is both simple to develop and easy for the listener to follow.

The Four Pages of the Sermon

A concept that has proven very helpful to us in moving from textual study to sermon creation has been Paul Scott Wilson's *The Four Pages of the Sermon*.

Despite its title, Wilson's 1999 book owes more to moviemaking than to literature for its inspiration. His idea is that a sermon needs to talk about two basic things: Trouble and Grace as they are active in two basic places, the Bible and the World.

Thus, what he calls the four pages of the sermon:

> 1) Trouble in the Bible,
>
> 2) Trouble in the World,
>
> 3) Grace (God's action) in the Bible, and
>
> 4) Grace in the World

Wilson says "The content of the four pages comes from the four kinds of material we can include in our sermons: basically, we are confined to talking about (1) sin and brokenness in the biblical world, (2) sin and brokenness in our world, (3) grace in the biblical world, and (4) grace in our world."

(Paul Scott Wilson, Nashville, Abingdon: *The Four Pages of the Sermon.*)

Wilson suggests that preachers should think like moviemakers and construct scenes about each of these themes, scenes that flow from one to the other to tell a **homiletical story** the way movies move from scene to scene to tell their cinematic stories.

"Thus, if we imagine that we are directing a film we allow ourselves to think and compose sermons in a visual manner - -which is how most of us think in any case." (Wilson, p. 11)

As we said, Wilson's technique is very helpful in making the move from the study to the pulpit. After one has done the normal biblical wrestling with the original languages and the texts and has a legal pad (or more likely these day, a laptop page) full of notes and ideas on the meaning of the text, the four pages of the sermon process becomes a way of sifting out what the text is doing in terms of the Bible's overarching redemptive story.

Take each of Wilson's questions in turn and seek out an answer. What is the "bad news" in this text? What is "the sin and brokenness" in this story?

Look at the world and ask, "What is the bad news in the world, where we are facing a similar sort of 'sin and brokenness' in our lives, in this town, in this church, in this time?"

And when that is answered, turn to the scripture for the remedy. "What is the good news in this text? Where is God's grace active in this story?"

Finally, ask, "Where can we see, or expect to see, or hope to see, God's grace active in our lives, here and now?"

When we have answered those questions we have a new plot, a new narrative. It is a narrative that is not shaped by the narrative plot line of the text but which does not do violence to it either. Nor is it shaped by a philosophical-logical progression but by the biblical mega-story progression from law to gospel, from sin to salvation.

Once you have your four pages, it becomes a simple matter to quickly arrange them to provide answers to our **Listener's Three Questions.**

> **What is the Problem?** There's trouble in the Bible, just as there's trouble in the world.

> **What is the answer?** There's grace in the Bible.

> **What difference does it make?** There is grace in the world – for each of us and for all of us.

This brings us back to where we started. No matter what form the preacher adopts, the listener's basic questions stay the same.

Our **Listener's Three Questions** model (like Lowry's *Homiletical Plot* and Wilson's *Four Pages of the Sermon*) is specifically **designed to make the sermon easy for the listener to hear and understand.**

The simplest way to preach, and the most effective, is to fit one's material into a form that works with the hearer's most natural way of listening.

In the next chapter, we'll consider how well the **Listener's Three Questions** might work with texts other than the gospel; i.e. will this work with something other than a narrative text?

Chapter Four: In Case You Were Wondering

"Okay, that **Listener's Three Questions** idea worked pretty well with a Gospel text, but how will it work with other types of biblical literature? What about one of the prophets, or a psalm, or readings from the epistles?"

We think it works pretty well. Every week on **The Lectionary Lab Live** podcast (www.lectionarylab.com) we review each of the lessons for the coming Sunday and frequently talk about preaching possibilities based on our basic method.

For example - here are the other lessons for **Proper 3, Year B** with a brief analysis of each using the **Listener's Three Questions**:

Hosea 2:14-20

14Therefore, I will now allure her, and bring her into the wilderness, and speak tenderly to her. 15From there I will give her her vineyards, and make the Valley of Achor a door of hope. There she shall respond as in the days of her youth, as at the time when she came out of the land of Egypt. 16On that day, says the Lord, you will call me, "My husband," and no longer will you call me, "My Baal." 17For I will remove the names of the Baals from her mouth, and they shall be mentioned by name no more. 18I will make for you a covenant on that day with the wild animals, the birds of the air, and the creeping things of the ground; and I will abolish the bow, the sword, and war from the land; and I will make you lie down in safety. 19And I will take you for my wife forever; I will take you for my wife in righteousness and in justice, in steadfast love, and in mercy. 20I will take you for my wife in faithfulness; and you shall know the Lord. 21On that day I will answer, says the Lord, I will answer the heavens and they shall answer the earth; 22and the earth shall answer the grain, the wine, and the oil, and they shall answer Jezreel; 23and I will sow him for myself in the land. And I will have pity on Lo-ruhamah, and I will say to Lo-ammi, "You are my people"; and he shall say, "You are my God."

What's the problem?

- The people are no longer being faithful to YHWH, they are beginning to worship BAAL

- The prophet makes the analogy of a straying spouse who cheats

- Modern world – is it people who are "spiritual but not religious" – or nominal church-members, who profess faith on Sunday but live as if there is no God the rest of the week, or who have perhaps confused the invisible hand of the market with the Lord God Almighty?

What's the answer?

- Hosea portrays the divine/human relationship as a marriage, a covenant of love, loyalty, tenderness, and commitment; not one of legalistic binding and heartless duty.

- God is a faithful spouse who stands ready to receive us back at any time we are ready to return – not judging and dismissing, but waiting and receiving.

- Key line: "I will . . . make the Valley of Achor a door of hope." Verse 15

- Valley of Achor means "Valley of Trouble" – literally a route up from Jericho to the hill country; Hosea uses it as a beautiful metaphor for finding our way back to a God who waits on the other side of our wandering troubles.

What difference does it make?

- There is always hope for any of us. God both actively seeks and patiently waits.

- The church is called to be a place that seeks and waits, invites and welcomes people back.

Psalm 103:1-13, 22

[1]Bless the Lord, O my soul, and all that is within me, bless his holy name.

²Bless the Lord, O my soul, and do not forget all his benefits—

³who forgives all your iniquity, who heals all your diseases,

⁴who redeems your life from the Pit, who crowns you with steadfast love and mercy,

⁵who satisfies you with good as long as you live so that your youth is renewed like the eagle's.

⁶The Lord works vindication and justice for all who are oppressed.

⁷He made known his ways to Moses, his acts to the people of Israel.

⁸The Lord is merciful and gracious, slow to anger and abounding in steadfast love.

⁹He will not always accuse, nor will he keep his anger forever.

¹⁰He does not deal with us according to our sins, nor repay us according to our iniquities.

¹¹For as the heavens are high above the earth, so great is his steadfast love toward those who fear him;

¹²as far as the east is from the west, so far he removes our transgressions from us.

¹³As a father has compassion for his children, so

the Lord has compassion for those who fear him.

[22]Bless the Lord, all his works, in all places of his dominion. Bless the Lord, O my soul.

What's the problem?

- Sin and forgetfulness. People sin and forget that God forgives and restores sinners.

- Modern world? People are more likely to think in terms of meaninglessness or a sense of failure and separation from God and others.

What's the answer?

- Remembering what God has done in the past.

- This is both individual remembering (1-5) and community remembering (6-7) of God's mighty acts of forgiveness and rescue. Based on these – we know that God is compassionate and forgiving. (8-10)

What difference does it make?

- We can turn to God in our troubles with trust that we will be welcomed with arms of love

- As the church, we are called to be a place where people hear about God's love and experience God's forgiveness, acceptance and compassion. (11-13, 22)

2 Corinthians 3:1-6

1 Are we beginning to commend ourselves again?
Surely we do not need, as some do, letters of
recommendation to you or from you, do we? [2]You
yourselves are our letter, written on our hearts, to be
known and read by all; [3]and you show that you are a
letter of Christ, prepared by us, written not with ink but
with the Spirit of the living God, not on tablets of stone
but on tablets of human hearts.

[4]Such is the confidence that we have through Christ
toward God. [5]Not that we are competent of ourselves
to claim anything as coming from us; our competence is
from God, [6]who has made us competent to be ministers
of a new covenant, not of letter but of spirit; for the
letter kills, but the Spirit gives life.

What's the problem?

- Distrust has grown up between Paul and some
  of the leadership of the church in Corinth.

- As often happens when human relationships
  break down, appeals are being made to rules
  and paper trails.

- In modern world, in churches, in work-places, in
  marriages, in politics; when we have nothing
  left but the letter of the law, we have no trust
  left in the relationship.

What's the answer?

- Twofold – remembrance of past relationship (2-3) and the Spirit working in both parties, (3,6) Key line is 6 – "the letter kills, but the Spirit gives life."

- "Back away from *Roberts Rules of Order* and the Church Constitution and let's talk and pray about this first."

What difference does it make?

- All churches, all work places, all volunteer groups, all marriages, all relationships go through times of distrust and misunderstanding.

- This text can be a reminder to us to dig deep into our history together to find that place of initial trust from which to rebuild our faith in each other.

- In the church and in our personal lives, this can take an overt form of appealing to prayer and God.

- In the more public forums of work and politics, it may require Christians to be peacemakers and reconcilers; trusting the Spirit and imitating Christ without directly identifying the religious basis of our actions.

Chapter Five: A Few Words about Stories

People like stories. They pay attention when speakers tell stories. And stories certainly fill up a lot of space in a sermon, which reduces theme development, which, in turn, shortens sermon preparation time.

If you preach a fifteen-minute sermon and tell a couple of five-minute stories, all you have left are a couple of minutes of introduction and conclusion and a bridge section in the middle from one story to the other. There are lots of places on the internet where one can find several appropriate and timely stories.

Alas, sermon preparation can become a desperate search for two or three usable stories that one can string together in a semi-ordered sequence. Some preachers just tell one long story without mentioning the text or the gospel, leaving the listener to make connections all on their own.

What many have failed to do is the hard work of figuring out how to use stories to bring about a genuine encounter between the hearer and the Biblical text. Here are a few basic guidelines and insights about using stories in sermons; personal stories in particular.

First of all, personal stories work best in the beginning section of the sermon, the **What's the Question?**

discussion. (See the previous chapter for the **Listener's Three Questions**.) There are a couple of reasons for this.

- **Stories are non-threatening.** Fred Craddock began *Overhearing the Gospel* with a quotation from Kierkegaard, "There is no lack of information in a Christian land; something else is lacking, and this is a something which the one man cannot directly communicate to the other." (Craddock, Fred B. *Overhearing the Gospel* [Nashville, Abingdon, 1978] p. 3) Personal story is non-threatening, does not directly communicate and allows people to "overhear" what the preacher has to say.

- **Stories help people get to know you.** Pastors and their congregations are less personally acquainted with one another than they used to be. A recent study shows that while 20 years ago most laypeople counted 2-3 times a month as "regular church attendance," more recent studies show that many people now count once a month as regular.

Homiletics professor and writer Calvin Miller made reference to the importance of the **pre-sermon**, especially for those who preach to congregations who don't know them well. (Miller, Calvin H., *Preaching: the Art of Narrative Exposition* [Grand Rapids, Baker, 2006] pp.41ff.)

By the pre-sermon, he means a few minutes of personal interaction for the speaker and the congregation to get comfortable with one another. Pastors who have many congregants whom they may not see more than 10-15 times a year are well served to aware of this dynamic. Beginning the sermon with a brief personal story that is also tied closely to the biblical narrative is a way to do this rather unobtrusively.

Some Do's and Don'ts of Telling Stories in Sermons

Storytelling has a lot in common with jokes and humor; some things simply do not translate across cultures. We cannot teach you how to tell a story, especially not a personal story that will work in your context. But essentially every culture tells stories and loves stories and you can learn by paying attention to the natural style of those around you.

We can tell you that in almost any culture, simpler is better than complex, linear timelines are easier to follow, and sharp vivid details are better than elaborate descriptive adjectives.

We can also tell you some things not to do, in any culture.

- **It is important in any story that you tell that you not be the hero**. Besides the fact that humility is a Christian virtue, Christ is the center of our Christian story and, "We preach not ourselves, but Jesus Christ as Lord . . ." (*2 Corinthians 4:5.)* While we would not say that talking about oneself in the sermon is "preaching ourselves," we do think that presenting ourselves as hero violates the need to keep Christ as Lord at the center of our proclamation.

- **It is also important not to be an "anti-hero," for this can be another way of drawing attention away from Christ and to yourself.** In the evangelistic churches of our youth, it sometimes seemed like the preachers were competing to see who had been the biggest sinner prior to their conversion. Confession is good for the soul, but not from the pulpit, at least not more than once or twice in a career and then only when it is the congregation that has been sinned against.

- **It is never a good idea to tell stories involving people in the congregation or people known to people in the congregation** (this includes your immediate family members) without their explicit permission. It may not be a good idea with their permission unless you tell the congregation "I have Mr. Smith's permission to tell you this story." And even then it has several dangers inherent in it; chief of which is that parishioners have a right to expect that you will keep their confidences. If stories of cute things and poignant conversations with parishioners keep popping up in your sermons, people will, consciously or unconsciously, shy away from you.

- **Don't use personal stories every week**. Sprinkle them into your sermon writing like a garnish on a well-cooked meal. Occasionally, it sparks interest; constantly, it becomes a problem. No hard and fast rule is possible, but about one out of every four or five sermons, and not on an "it's-the-third-Sunday-time-for-a-personal-story" timetable. One of our former colleagues was always fond of the saying, "If the only tool you have is a hammer, every problem looks suspiciously like a nail." Let personal story be a tool, but not your only tool, and only use it when the occasion calls for it. Having given those warnings, there are some good reasons to use personal story and some good ways to do; and these reasons and techniques are tied together.

- **Preaching is the product of a personal encounter** of the preacher with a particular part of the biblical story in the context of being called to speak this unique Word of God to a particular group of people. It is a very personal event and to pretend otherwise is to create a false distance between the self and the preaching event.

- **Preaching presumes that God-in-Christ is still actively involved in reconciling the world to**

God's self, and that this activity is perceptible in people's lives, including the preacher's life. Therefore, the preachers should pay attention to such God-moments in their lives and appropriately share those moments with their hearers. The important thing to remember is that it is God who is the actor in these stories, encountering our lives, reconciling us to God and each other.

- **In terms of Fred Craddock's views on "Overhearing the Gospel," the best way for folks to overhear the Gospel is to see the gospel intersecting a normal life similar to their own**. They don't need to hear "hero" stories or "anti-hero" stories. They need to hear about ordinary efforts to make sense of life in the light of the biblical story. Therefore, it is the job of the preacher to think theologically about his or her very own very ordinary life, to be "the common person" with theologically-trained eyes and ears.

Allow us to close with a word from one of our favorite storytellers, **C.S. Lewis**, reportedly from a sermon preached in St. Jude on the Hill Church in London, on November 26th, 1942. It captures for us something of the miracle of preaching to our people week after week.

"Miracles are a retelling in small letters of the very same story which is written across the whole world in letters too large for some of us to see."

-- C.S. Lewis, *God in the Dock* (Eerdmans, 1972)

Appendix: Helpful Resources

Help with Greek and Hebrew

www.biblehub.com

This website, a production of the **Online Parallel Bible Project**, contains a number of excellent tools and resources for in-depth scripture study. The Interlinear versions of particular Bible texts allow you to click and explore words in the original biblical languages with helpful English translations, pronunciation guides, word origin studies, and much more. Definitely worth a bookmark on your computer!

The Hebrew-Greek Key Word Study Bible, edited by Dr. Spiros Zodhiates and Dr. Warren Patrick Baker (AMG Publishers, various versions and dates.)

For those who prefer to hold a "real book," this excellent tool by the late Spiros Zodhiates is eminently useful. Based on either KJV, NIV, or NASB translations, there is a numbered system of cross-references and dictionaries of the Hebrew and Greek words used in scripture. With a little diligence, one can get at the essential meanings of the texts in these original languages, even if you have never taken Greek or Hebrew.

For Further Reading

David Buttrick: *Homiletic – Moves and Structures*
(Fortress Press, 1987.)

> The most helpful thing we learned from this
> volume is "how sermons form in consciousness and
> how the language of preaching functions in the
> communal consciousness of a congregation."

Fred Craddock: *Overhearing the Gospel*
(Revised and Expanded) Chalice Press, 2002

> Still the best thing available on paying attention to
> how people listen so that you can shape your
> preaching into a form they can hear.

Eugene L. Lowry: *The Homiletical Beat: Why All
Sermons are Narrative.* (Abingdon Press, 2012.)

> Lowry updates his *Homiltical Plot* in this volume,
> which is based on his 2009 Lyman Beecher Lecture
> on Preaching at Yale.

Paul Scott Wilson: *The Four Pages of the Sermon: A
Guide to Biblical Preaching.* (Abingdon Press, 1999.)

> Clarifies two things very well: 1) how to sort your
> material into preachable units, and 2) how to write
> scenes instead of points.

ABOUT THE AUTHORS

Delmer Chilton is a native of North Carolina and attended the University of North Carolina, Duke Divinity School, Lutheran Theological Southern Seminary, and the Graduate Theological Foundation. He is a Lutheran pastor serving as Priest-in-Charge of the Episcopal Church of the Messiah in Murphy, North Carolina.

John Fairless is a Tennessean who attended the University of Tennessee, Southern Baptist Theological Seminary, Vanderbilt Divinity School, and Princeton Theological Seminary, He is the Senior Pastor of the First Baptist Church of Gainesville, Florida.

* * * * * * *

Known by friends and colleagues as *Two Bubbas and a Bible*, John and Delmer write a weekly lectionary commentary and produce a weekly podcast discussing the texts for the upcoming Sunday. Both are available on their main website, www.lectionarylab.com.

Made in the USA
Lexington, KY
08 November 2014